Kreye Art Studio

May, 2024

Trading Rules

ABC Trading Rules

A Clear, Simple System for Consistent Forex Success

by

Tagi-Alum; Bey

Kreye Art Studio Publishing

www.kreyeart.com

ABC Trading Rules

For permission requests, contact:

Kreye Art Studio Publishing

www.kreyeart.com

ISBN: 979-8227283672

Cover & Layout Design by **Kreye Art Studio**

This book is for educational purposes only. Trading in the financial markets involves risk. Past performance is not indicative of future results. Always trade responsibly and seek professional advice when needed.

Table Of Contents

1. Introduction...5-6

2. Jack And The Magical Trading Adventure...7-9

3. ABC Trading Rules A-C....................................10-21

4. ABC Trading Rules D-G..................................22-33

5. ABC Trading Rules H-K..................................35-45

6. ABC Trading Rules L-O..................................46-59

7. ABC Trading Rules P-S...................................60-71

8. ABC Trading Rules T-W 72-83

9. ABC Trading Rules XYZ..................................84-93

10. Conclusion..94-98

Introduction

Welcome to the vibrant world of creativity, entrepreneurship, and financial markets – where artistry meets innovation, and dreams take flight. I am Tagi-Alum; Bey, I reserve all of my rights, at all times, i trade currency pairs, and I'm an artist hailing from the bustling city of Nashville, Tennessee. From the soulful melodies of country music to the eclectic energy of its art scene, Nashville has always been my muse, inspiring me to explore the boundless realms of creativity.

As an artist, I've always been drawn to the power of visual expression. Whether it's capturing the raw beauty of nature on canvas or infusing life into digital designs, I've found solace and inspiration in the act of creation. What started as a passion project soon blossomed into a full-fledged graphic design company, where I have the privilege of bringing my clients visions to life through innovative design solutions.

But my journey doesn't end there. Alongside my endeavors in the creative realm, I've also embarked on a thrilling adventure in the

world of finance – specifically, the foreign exchange market. With a keen eye for patterns and a thirst for knowledge, I've honed my skills as a trader, navigating the complexities of the forex market with precision and finesse.

But I'm not alone in this journey. I trade with a prop firm, where I'm surrounded by like-minded individuals who share my passion for the markets and drive for success. Together, we leverage our collective expertise and resources to seize opportunities and overcome challenges, propelling ourselves toward greater heights of achievement.

In this book, I invite you to join me on a journey of exploration and discovery – a journey that transcends boundaries and embraces the intersection of art, entrepreneurship, and trading. Whether you're a fellow artist seeking inspiration, an aspiring entrepreneur with dreams of building your own empire, or a curious soul intrigued by the world of finance, there's something here for you. That you may share with your children, childrens, grand children.

So come, let us embark on this adventure together, as we uncover the secrets of success right now, unlock the power of creativity, and chart a course toward a future filled with endless possibilities.

Jack and his *Magical Trading Adventure*

Once upon a time, in a cozy house on the outskirts of East Nashville, Tennessee, there lived an adventurous 9-year-old boy named Jack. With a sparkle in his eye and a heart full of wonder, Jack loved nothing more than exploring the world around him, always on the lookout for exciting new adventures.

Jack's dad, Mr. James, was a businessman who often went on trips for work, leaving Jack and his mom at home. One sunny Friday afternoon, as Mr. James packed his bags for yet another trip, Jack couldn't help but feel a little sad. He wished he could go on adventures like his dad.

As Jack watched his dad getting ready, he noticed his shiny iPhone lying on the kitchen counter. Jack had seen his dad use it to make calls and send emails, but he had never really operated it by himself.

With a mischievous grin, Jack's imagination started to run wild.

While his dad was busy packing, Jack sneaked over to the counter and grabbed the iPhone. He knew he wasn't supposed to touch it without permission, but the temptation was too great. With a sense of excitement bubbling inside him, Jack hurried back to his room to explore.

Sitting cross-legged on his bed, Jack began tapping and swiping at the screen, marveling at all the colorful buttons and pictures. But as he played around, something strange happened. Without realizing it, Jack accidentally opened a special app that he had never seen before – a magical trading game!

Suddenly, Jack found himself surrounded by charts and numbers, with buttons that promised to make exciting things happen. Not knowing what to do, Jack started pressing buttons at random, his heart racing with excitement.

To his amazement, each button he pressed seemed to make something magical happen. Colors flashed, numbers changed, and before he knew it, Jack was making trades on the foreign exchange market – a place where people buy and sell money from different countries!

At first, Jack was scared. He didn't know what he was doing, and he was worried he might mess something up. But as he kept

playing, he started to understand how everything worked. With each trade he made, Jack's confidence grew stronger.

As the sun began to set and Jack's dad's business trip came to an end, Jack realized something amazing. By accident, he had learned how to trade on the foreign exchange market, and he had made some incredible trades!

With a proud smile on his face, Jack rushed to show his dad what he had done. When Mr. James saw how smart and brave his son had been, he couldn't believe it. He hugged Jack tight and told him how proud he was.

From that day on, Jack and his dad became trading buddies, learning and exploring together. And as they embarked on countless adventures in the magical world of trading, Jack knew that he had found a special kind of magic – the magic of learning, growing, and believing in himself.

And so, with a heart full of wonder and a spirit full of courage, Jack's journey into the world of trading had only just begun.

A. Do NOT risk more than 1% of your account balance.

The *Golden Rule* of Risk Management

In Jack's adventure, he initially didn't understand the risks involved in trading and accidentally risked his father's money without fully comprehending the consequences. However, as Jack learned more about trading, he realized the importance of risk management and began to apply the 1% rule to his trades. By limiting his risk exposure, Jack ***protected*** *his capital and* ***ensured*** *that no single trade could wipe out his account.*

Introduction

In the fast-paced world of trading, one rule stands tall as the cornerstone of success: never risk more than 1% of your account balance on any single trade. In this chapter, we'll explore why this rule is sacrosanct, how it forms the bedrock of sound risk management, and why it's the key to safeguarding your capital in the tumultuous waters of the financial markets.

Exploration

1. *Capital Preservation*: At its core, the 1% rule is about protecting what matters most – your capital. By limiting the amount you risk on each trade, you ensure that no single loss can decimate your account. This preservation of capital is not just prudent; it's essential for your long-term survival as a trader.

2. *Risk vs. Reward:* Trading is a game of probabilities, and the 1% rule helps you play it smart. By carefully balancing risk and reward, you ensure that your potential losses are always dwarfed by your potential gains. This asymmetrical risk-reward profile is the hallmark of successful traders.

3. *Emotional Discipline:* Trading can be an emotional rollercoaster, with highs and lows that can cloud your judgment. The 1% rule acts as a bulwark against emotional decision-making, providing a clear, rational framework for managing risk. When you know that no single trade can make or break your account, you're free to trade with confidence and discipline.

4. *Consistency and Longevity*: Consistency is the key to long-term success in trading, and the 1% rule is your ticket to consistency. By adhering to this rule day in and day out, trade after trade, you build a solid foundation for sustainable growth. You may not hit home runs with every trade, but over time, the steady accumulation of gains will propel you toward your financial goals.

5. *Adaptability:* Markets are dynamic, and trading strategies must evolve to keep pace. The 1% rule is not a one-size-fits-all solution; it's a principle that adapts to your changing circumstances and market conditions. Whether you're a seasoned pro or a novice trader, this rule remains your guiding light in the ever-shifting landscape of trading.

Conclusion

In the unpredictable world of trading, the only certainty is uncertainty. But amidst the chaos, one rule shines through as a beacon of clarity: never risk more than 1% of your account balance. This rule is more than just a guideline; it's a philosophy, a mindset, a way of life. By embracing it wholeheartedly, you'll not only protect your capital but also unlock the door to consistent, sustainable success in the markets.

Here are some quick and insightful **tips** derived from each trading rule that YOU can implement immediately:

A. **Do not risk more than 1% of your account balance:**

- *Calculate the 1% risk for each trade based on your account size before entering any position.*

- *Set stop-loss orders at appropriate levels to limit potential losses within the 1% risk threshold.*

B. **Once your TP & SL is set, leave it there:**

- *Resist the temptation to adjust stop-loss or take-profit levels based on short-term market fluctuations.*

- *Trust your initial analysis and trading plan, and allow the trade to play out according to your predefined parameters*

B. Once your TP & SL is set, leave it there.

The *Art* of Patience

As Jack continued his trading journey, he encountered the challenge of setting Take Profit (TP) and Stop Loss (SL) levels and resisting the temptation to adjust them impulsively. Through trial and error, Jack learned the importance of sticking to his original plan and leaving TP and SL levels unchanged once they were set. This disciplined approach helped Jack avoid emotional decision-making and stay true to his trading strategy.

Introduction

In the fast-paced world of trading, patience is a virtue that can make all the difference between success and failure. Rule B – Once your Take Profit (TP) and Stop Loss (SL) is set, leave it there – embodies the essence of this principle. In this chapter, we'll delve into the art of patience and explore why sticking to your trading plan without succumbing to impulsive decisions is key to long-term profitability.

Exploration

1. *Discipline and Consistency*: Setting TP and SL levels is a crucial aspect of risk management and trade planning. Once these levels are determined based on your strategy, it's essential to exercise discipline and consistency by leaving them unchanged. This steadfast approach ensures that your trades are guided by a predetermined plan rather than influenced by emotional reactions to market fluctuations.

2. *Avoiding Emotional Decision-Making*: Emotions can run high in the midst of market volatility, leading traders to second-guess their decisions and make impulsive changes to their trades. By adhering to Rule B, traders mitigate the risk of falling prey to emotional decision-making. This allows them to maintain a rational and objective mindset, even in the face of adversity.

3. *Respecting Risk Management*: TP and SL levels are integral components of a trader's risk management strategy. By adhering to these levels and leaving them unchanged, traders ensure that their risk-reward ratio remains intact. This disciplined approach helps to protect trading capital and minimize losses, ultimately contributing to long-term profitability.

4. *Trust in Your Strategy*: Rule B reinforces the importance of trusting in your trading strategy and allowing it to play out without interference. By leaving TP and SL levels untouched, traders demonstrate confidence in their analysis and decision-making process. This trust fosters a sense of self-assurance and consistency, which are essential qualities for success in the markets.

5. *Learning from Experience*: Over time, traders may be tempted to tinker with TP and SL levels based on past experiences or market conditions. However, Rule B encourages traders to learn from their experiences and stick to their original plan. Whether a trade ends in profit or loss, there are valuable lessons to be gleaned from every outcome, reinforcing the importance of discipline and patience.

Conclusion

In the dynamic world of trading, patience is not just a virtue – it's a necessity. Rule B – Once your TP & SL is set, leave it there – serves as a guiding principle that underscores the importance of discipline, consistency, and trust in one's trading strategy. By adhering to this rule, traders can navigate the complexities of the market with confidence, knowing that their decisions are grounded in sound analysis and unwavering discipline.

Here are some quick and insightful **tips** derived from each trading rule that YOU can implement immediately:

A. Do not risk more than 1% of your account balance:

- Calculate the 1% risk for each trade based on your account size before entering any position.

- Set stop-loss orders at appropriate levels to limit potential losses within the 1% risk threshold.

B. Once your TP & SL is set, leave it there:

- Resist the temptation to adjust stop-loss or take-profit levels based on short-term market fluctuations.

- Trust your initial analysis and trading plan, and allow the trade to play out according to your predefined parameters

C. If you lose two trades, call it a day.

Knowing When To Step Back

In Jack's adventure, he experienced setbacks and losses along the way, but he quickly learned the importance of knowing when to step back and take a break. By implementing the rule of calling it a day after two consecutive losses, Jack prevented himself from making impulsive decisions fueled by frustration or the desire to recoup losses. Instead, he gave himself time to regroup, recharge, and approach the markets with a fresh perspective.

Introduction

Trading can be a rollercoaster of highs and lows, and knowing when to step back is a skill that separates successful traders from the rest. Rule C – If you lose two trades, call it a day – highlights the importance of recognizing when it's time to take a break and regroup. In this chapter, we'll explore the art of knowing when to step back and the benefits it brings to a trader's mindset and performance.

Exploration

1. Preserving Mental Capital: Trading is not just about preserving financial capital; it's also about preserving mental capital. After

experiencing two consecutive losses, emotions can run high, and decision-making can become clouded. Calling it a day allows traders to step back from the intensity of the markets and preserve their mental well-being.

2. *Preventing Emotional Decision-Making*: Emotions can be a trader's worst enemy, leading to impulsive decisions and irrational behavior. By implementing Rule C, traders prevent themselves from making emotional decisions in the heat of the moment. Stepping back after two losses provides a cooling-off period, allowing traders to regain perspective and approach the markets with a clear mind.

3. *Avoiding Revenge Trading*: Revenge trading, or the urge to recoup losses by immediately entering new trades, is a common pitfall for many traders. Rule C serves as a safeguard against revenge trading by imposing a limit on the number of consecutive losses a trader can experience in a single day. By calling it a day after two losses, traders avoid the temptation to chase losses and potentially dig themselves into a deeper hole.

4. *Maintaining Discipline*: Discipline is the cornerstone of successful trading, and Rule C reinforces this principle. By adhering to a predefined rule regarding when to stop trading,

traders demonstrate discipline and commitment to their trading plan. This consistency builds confidence and trust in one's ability to navigate the markets effectively.

5. *Fostering a Positive Mindset*: Trading is as much a mental game as it is a strategic one. By calling it a day after two losses, traders avoid dwelling on negative outcomes and instead focus on maintaining a positive mindset. Stepping back allows traders to recharge, regroup, and come back to the markets with renewed energy and optimism.

Conclusion

Rule C – If you lose two trades, call it a day – is a powerful tool for preserving mental well-being, preventing emotional decision-making, and maintaining discipline in the face of adversity. By recognizing when it's time to step back and take a break, traders set themselves up for long-term success by ensuring that they approach the markets with clarity, composure, and confidence.

Here are some quick and insightful **tips** derived from each trading rule that YOU can implement immediately:

C. If you lose two trades, call it a day:

- Acknowledge when you're experiencing a losing streak and take a step back from trading to avoid emotional decision-making.

- Reflect on the reasons behind the losses and identify potential areas for improvement in your trading strategy.

D. If you lose three trades, call it a week.

While Jack didn't explicitly encounter the rule of calling it a week after three consecutive losses in his story, the concept of taking a longer break after a series of losses can still be applied. By giving himself time to reflect and learn from his experiences, Jack avoided the trap of overtrading and maintained a disciplined approach to his trading journey.

Exploration

1. *Managing Losing Streaks*: Rule D emphasizes the importance of recognizing when a trader is experiencing a prolonged losing streak and taking proactive steps to mitigate further losses. By calling it a week after three consecutive losing trades, traders can prevent emotional decision-making and avoid compounding losses by stepping back and reassessing their approach.

2. *Preserving Mental Capital*: Trading can be mentally taxing, especially during periods of sustained losses. By calling it a week after three losses, traders give themselves time to recharge and regain perspective, preserving their mental capital and preventing burnout. This disciplined approach fosters resilience and helps traders maintain a healthy mindset in the face of adversity.

3. *Avoiding Overtrading*: Overtrading is a common pitfall for many traders, particularly during periods of frustration or desperation following losses. Rule D acts as a safeguard against overtrading by imposing a limit on the number of losing trades a trader can endure within a specified timeframe. By calling it a week after three losses, traders avoid the temptation to chase losses and instead focus on regrouping and reassessing their strategy.

4. *Learning from Mistakes*: Losing trades are inevitable in trading, but they also present valuable learning opportunities. By calling it a week after three losses, traders give themselves time to reflect on their mistakes, identify areas for improvement, and adjust their approach accordingly. This reflective practice fosters growth and development, ultimately making traders more resilient and adaptable in the face of changing market conditions.

Conclusion

Rule D – If you lose three trades, call it a week – underscores the importance of recognizing and managing losing streaks in trading. By imposing a limit on the number of consecutive losses within a specified timeframe, traders can prevent emotional decision-making, preserve their mental capital, and foster a disciplined approach to their trading journey.

Here are some quick and insightful **tips** derived from each trading rule that YOU can implement immediately:

D. If you lose three trades, call it a week:

- *Take a break from trading for the rest of the week to prevent further losses and preserve capital.*

- *Use the time to review your trading journal, analyze past trades, and refine your approach for the following week.*

E. Only enter trades with the overall trend.

As Jack delved deeper into the world of trading, he discovered the importance of trading with the trend. While he initially made trades based on curiosity and experimentation, Jack soon realized that aligning his trades with the overall trend increased his probability of success. By following this rule, Jack capitalized on market momentum and minimized the risk of trading against the prevailing direction.

Exploration

1. *Aligning with Market Forces*: Rule E emphasizes the importance of trading in harmony with the prevailing market direction. The overall trend represents the dominant force driving price movements, and aligning with it increases the probability of trade success. By entering trades that follow the trend, traders position themselves on the side of market momentum, enhancing their chances of profiting from favorable price movements.

2. *Reducing Counter-Trend Risk*: Trading against the trend carries inherent risks, as counter-trend moves can be unpredictable and short-lived. Rule E mitigates this risk by encouraging traders to focus on trades that align with the broader market direction. By avoiding counter-trend trades, traders minimize the likelihood of

being caught on the wrong side of a sudden reversal and experiencing significant losses.

3. *Utilizing Trend-Following Strategies*: Trend-following strategies are among the most widely used and effective approaches in trading. Rule E aligns with this principle by guiding traders to seek opportunities that coincide with the established trend. Whether employing moving averages, trendlines, or other trend indicators, traders can leverage these tools to identify high-probability trades that align with the prevailing market sentiment.

4. *Maximizing Profit Potential*: Trading with the trend allows traders to capitalize on extended price moves in the direction of market momentum. By entering trades that align with the overall trend, traders aim to ride the trend for maximum profit potential, capturing substantial gains as prices continue to move in their favor. This approach emphasizes the importance of patience and discipline in allowing winning trades to run their course.

Conclusion

Rule E – Only enter trades with the overall trend – underscores the significance of aligning with market forces to enhance trade success. By focusing on trades that follow the prevailing market direction, traders minimize counter-trend risk, utilize trend-following strategies effectively, and maximize profit potential by capitalizing on extended price moves. This disciplined approach fosters consistency and confidence in traders' decision-making, leading to long-term success in the markets.

Here are some quick and insightful **tips** derived from each trading rule that YOU can implement immediately:

E. Only enter trades with the overall trend:

- *Use trend-following indicators such as moving averages, leading indicators, or trendlines to identify the direction of the prevailing trend.*

- *Wait for pullbacks or retracements within the trend to enter trades in the direction of the overall market bias.*

F. Do NOT enter a trade without three confluences.

In Jack's story, he learned the value of thorough analysis and multiple confirmations before entering a trade. While he initially made trades impulsively, Jack soon recognized the importance of waiting for three confluences – such as technical indicators, chart patterns, and fundamental factors – to align before executing a trade. This disciplined approach helped Jack filter out false signals and identify high-probability trading opportunities.

Exploration

1. Enhancing Trade Quality: Rule F emphasizes the importance of thorough analysis and confirmation before entering a trade. By requiring three confluences or confirming factors, traders ensure that their trades meet a higher standard of quality and reliability. This disciplined approach helps traders filter out false signals and focus on trades with a higher probability of success.

2. *Combining Multiple Perspectives:* Seeking three confluences encourages traders to consider multiple perspectives and sources of information before making a trading decision. Whether analyzing technical indicators, chart patterns, or fundamental factors, traders evaluate a variety of criteria to confirm the validity of a potential trade setup. This comprehensive approach reduces

the likelihood of entering trades based on isolated signals or incomplete information.

3. *Validating Trade Signals*: Confluences serve as validation points for trade signals, indicating a higher degree of agreement among different factors. When multiple indicators or signals align, they reinforce the conviction behind a trade idea and increase its reliability. Traders can have greater confidence in trades supported by multiple confluences, knowing that they have been thoroughly validated through comprehensive analysis.

4. *Minimizing False Signals*: False signals are a common challenge in trading, leading to losses and frustration for traders. Rule F mitigates this risk by requiring confirmation from three confluences before entering a trade. By demanding a higher threshold of evidence, traders reduce the likelihood of falling victim to false signals and increase their chances of identifying genuine trading opportunities.

Conclusion

Rule F – Do NOT enter a trade without three confluences – underscores the importance of comprehensive analysis and confirmation in trading. By seeking confirmation from multiple sources and perspectives, traders enhance trade quality, validate trade signals, and minimize the risk of false signals. This disciplined approach promotes consistency and reliability in trading decisions, ultimately contributing to long-term success in the markets.

Here are some quick and insightful **tips** derived from each trading rule that YOU can implement immediately:

F. Do not enter a trade without three confluences:

- Look for multiple technical indicators, chart patterns, or fundamental factors aligning to support your trade thesis.

- Avoid trading based on a single signal or indicator; seek confirmation from multiple sources before entering a position.

G. Only trade in your designated session.

Although Jack's story didn't explicitly address trading within a designated session, the concept of trading during optimal market conditions can still be applied. By focusing his trading activities during specific sessions with high liquidity and volatility, Jack maximized his chances of success and avoided trading during periods of low activity or erratic price movements.

Exploration

1. *Optimizing Trading Conditions*: Rule G emphasizes the importance of trading during designated sessions when market conditions are optimal. Each trading session has its unique characteristics, such as liquidity, volatility, and price movement patterns. By focusing on a specific session aligned with their trading strategy and preferences, traders can capitalize on favorable market conditions and avoid trading during periods of low activity or erratic price behavior.

2. *Reducing Overtrading*: Trading outside of designated sessions can increase the risk of overtrading, as traders may be tempted to enter positions impulsively in response to sporadic price movements. Rule G helps traders maintain discipline by restricting trading activities to specific times when they are most likely to

achieve their trading objectives. By adhering to a structured schedule, traders avoid the pitfalls of overtrading and maintain a focused approach to their trading activities.

3. *Enhancing Focus and Concentration*: Trading during designated sessions allows traders to allocate their time and energy more effectively, enhancing their focus and concentration during active market hours. By eliminating distractions and honing their attention on specific trading opportunities, traders can make better-informed decisions and execute trades with greater precision and confidence.

4. *Adapting to Market Dynamics*: Different trading sessions correspond to varying market dynamics, influenced by factors such as overlapping trading hours, economic releases, and geopolitical events. Rule G encourages traders to align their trading activities with these market dynamics, enabling them to capitalize on price movements driven by specific catalysts or market participants. By staying attuned to market sentiment and activity during designated sessions, traders can adapt their strategies accordingly and optimize their trading performance.

Conclusion

Rule G – Only trade in your designated session – underscores the importance of trading discipline and aligning with optimal market conditions. By focusing on specific trading sessions suited to their trading style and objectives, traders can minimize the risk of overtrading, enhance their focus and concentration, and adapt to market dynamics more effectively. This disciplined approach fosters consistency and precision in trading decisions, leading to improved performance and outcomes in the markets.

Here are some quick and insightful **tips** derived from each trading rule that YOU can implement immediately:

. **G. Only trade in your designated session:**

- *Identify the most active and liquid trading sessions for your chosen instrument and focus on trading during those times.*

- *Avoid trading during low-volume or overlapping sessions, as market conditions may be less predictable.*

H. Enter trades with a 1:3 risk reward ratio or higher.

As Jack continued to refine his trading strategy, he learned the importance of seeking trades with a favorable risk-reward ratio. By aiming for a ratio of 1:3 or higher – where the potential reward outweighed the risk by at least three times – Jack ensured that his trades had the potential to yield significant profits while keeping losses manageable. This prudent approach to risk management contributed to Jack's long-term success in the markets.

Exploration

1. Emphasizing Risk-Reward Ratio: Rule H highlights the significance of the risk-reward ratio in trade planning and decision-making. A risk-reward ratio of 1:3 means that for every unit of risk (e.g., one percent of the trading account), the potential reward is three times greater. By adhering to this rule, traders aim to achieve a favorable balance between risk and reward, ensuring that potential profits outweigh potential losses.

2. *Protecting Trading Capital*: Maintaining a favorable risk-reward ratio is essential for protecting trading capital and managing risk

effectively. Rule H encourages traders to prioritize trades that offer a sufficient reward relative to the amount of risk undertaken. By seeking trades with a minimum risk-reward ratio of 1:3, traders minimize the impact of losing trades on their overall account balance and preserve capital for future trading opportunities.

3. *Maximizing Profit Potential*: A high risk-reward ratio enables traders to capitalize on profitable opportunities and maximize their profit potential over time. By targeting trades with a minimum reward three times greater than the risk, traders ensure that winning trades contribute significantly to their overall profitability, outweighing the impact of any individual losing trades. This disciplined approach emphasizes the importance of patience and selective trade selection to achieve long-term success in trading.

4. *Enhancing Consistency*: Consistently applying a 1:3 risk-reward ratio to trades reinforces disciplined trade management and decision-making. By adhering to this rule, traders develop a systematic approach to evaluating trade opportunities and assessing their potential risk and reward. This consistency fosters confidence in trading decisions and promotes a disciplined mindset, essential qualities for achieving consistent profitability in the markets.

Conclusion

Rule H – Enter trades with a 1:3 risk-reward ratio or higher – underscores the importance of risk management and reward maximization in trading. By prioritizing trades that offer a favorable risk-reward ratio of at least 1:3, traders protect their capital, maximize profit potential, and enhance consistency in their trading results. This disciplined approach promotes prudent risk management and strategic decision-making, contributing to long-term success and sustainability in the markets.

Here are some quick and insightful **tips** derived from each trading rule that YOU can implement immediately:

H. Enter trades with a 1:3 risk reward ratio or higher:

- *Calculate the potential reward-to-risk ratio before entering a trade to ensure that the potential profit outweighs the potential loss.*

- *Set take-profit levels at least three times larger than your initial stop-loss level to maintain a favorable risk-reward profile.*

I. Trade currency pairs only.

In Jack's journey, he discovered the benefits of focusing his trading efforts exclusively on currency pairs. While he initially dabbled in various markets out of curiosity, Jack soon realized that specializing in currency pairs allowed him to develop a deeper understanding of their unique characteristics and behavior. By honing his skills within a specific asset class, Jack became a more informed and confident trader.

Exploration

1. *Specialization and Focus*: Rule I emphasizes the importance of specialization and focus in trading. Currency pairs represent one of the most liquid and actively traded asset classes in the financial markets. By limiting trading activities to currency pairs, traders can develop expertise in analyzing and understanding the unique characteristics and behavior of these instruments. Specialization allows traders to deepen their understanding of currency market dynamics and make more informed trading decisions.

2. *Capitalizing on Forex Market Opportunities*: The foreign exchange (forex) market offers a wide range of trading opportunities, including major currency pairs, crosses, and exotic pairs. Rule I encourages traders to capitalize on the diverse

opportunities available in the forex market by focusing exclusively on currency pairs. By trading forex exclusively, traders gain exposure to various global economies, geopolitical events, and monetary policies, enabling them to profit from currency fluctuations and volatility.

3. *Leveraging Liquidity and Volatility*: Currency pairs are known for their high liquidity and volatility, making them attractive instruments for traders seeking opportunities for profit. Rule I encourages traders to leverage the liquidity and volatility of currency pairs to execute trades with ease and capitalize on price movements. By trading in the forex market, traders can access deep liquidity pools and benefit from tight spreads, facilitating efficient trade execution and minimizing transaction costs.

4. *Managing Risk*: Focusing on currency pairs allows traders to effectively manage risk and exposure in their trading portfolios. Unlike other asset classes that may exhibit correlation or interdependence, currency pairs often move independently of other financial instruments. Rule I enables traders to diversify their risk across different currency pairs, reducing the impact of adverse market movements on their overall trading performance. Additionally, trading currency pairs exclusively allows traders to

implement risk management strategies tailored to the unique characteristics of the forex market.

Conclusion

Rule I – Trade currency pairs only – underscores the benefits of specialization, focus, and opportunity in the forex market. By limiting trading activities to currency pairs, traders can deepen their understanding of market dynamics, capitalize on diverse trading opportunities, and effectively manage risk in their trading portfolios. This disciplined approach fosters expertise, efficiency, and profitability in forex trading, positioning traders for long-term success and sustainability in the dynamic currency markets.

Here are some quick and insightful **tips** derived from each trading rule that YOU can implement immediately:

I. Trade currency pairs only:

- Focus on mastering the behavior and characteristics of a few select currency pairs rather than trading multiple instruments.

- Develop a deep understanding of the fundamental drivers and market dynamics specific to each currency pair you trade

J. Make sure you do not revenge trade.

As Jack faced challenges and setbacks in his trading journey, he learned the dangers of revenge trading – the urge to recoup losses by immediately entering new trades. By recognizing this temptation and resisting the impulse to chase losses, Jack avoided making emotional decisions that could further damage his trading account. Instead, he remained disciplined and focused on following his trading plan.

Exploration

1. *Emotional Discipline*: Rule J emphasizes the importance of emotional discipline and resilience in trading. Revenge trading occurs when traders attempt to recoup losses by immediately entering new trades without a sound trading plan or analysis. This impulsive behavior is driven by emotions such as frustration, anger, or a desire for redemption after experiencing losses. Rule J encourages traders to avoid revenge trading by maintaining emotional control and adhering to their trading strategy, even in the face of setbacks.

2. *Objective Decision-Making*: Revenge trading compromises traders' ability to make objective and rational decisions. Instead of following a systematic approach based on analysis and risk

management, revenge traders react impulsively to emotions and external stimuli. Rule J reminds traders to prioritize objective decision-making and avoid allowing emotions to dictate their trading actions. By staying disciplined and focused on their trading plan, traders can minimize the risk of revenge trading and its detrimental effects on their trading performance.

3. *Mitigating Further Losses*: Revenge trading often leads to a cycle of escalating losses, as traders compound their initial losses with additional unsuccessful trades. Rule J seeks to break this cycle by urging traders to step back and reassess their approach after experiencing losses. By avoiding revenge trading and taking a disciplined approach to trade management, traders can mitigate further losses and protect their trading capital from significant drawdowns.

4. *Staying True to Trading Strategy*: Revenge trading deviates from traders' established trading strategies and undermines their long-term goals and objectives. Rule J reinforces the importance of staying true to one's trading strategy and maintaining consistency in trading decisions. By adhering to a well-defined trading plan based on analysis, risk management, and discipline, traders can avoid the pitfalls of revenge trading and maintain a focused and disciplined approach to their trading activities.

Conclusion

Rule J – Make sure you do not revenge trade – underscores the importance of emotional discipline and objective decision-making in trading. By avoiding revenge trading and maintaining control over their emotions, traders can protect their trading capital, mitigate further losses, and stay true to their trading strategy. This disciplined approach fosters consistency, resilience, and long-term success in the challenging and dynamic environment of the financial markets.

Here are some quick and insightful **tips** derived from each trading rule that YOU can implement immediately:

J. Make sure you do not revenge trade:

- *Recognize when emotions are driving your trading decisions, especially after experiencing a loss.*

- *Take a break, practice mindfulness techniques, or seek support from a trading mentor to avoid succumbing to revenge trading impulses.*

K. Never ever force a trade.

In Jack's adventure, he experienced moments of uncertainty and hesitation when considering whether to enter a trade. However, he soon realized that forcing trades out of impatience or FOMO (Fear Of Missing Out) often led to suboptimal outcomes. By exercising patience and waiting for high-probability trading opportunities to present themselves, Jack avoided the pitfalls of forcing trades and maintained a disciplined approach to his trading strategy.

Exploration

1. Patience and Discipline: Rule K emphasizes the importance of patience and discipline in trading. Forcing a trade occurs when traders enter positions impulsively or out of boredom, rather than based on a well-defined trading plan or analysis. This behavior often leads to suboptimal trading outcomes and unnecessary losses. Rule K reminds traders to exercise patience and discipline, waiting for high-probability trading opportunities that align with their strategy and criteria.

2. *Quality over Quantity*: Forcing trades prioritizes quantity over quality, which can be detrimental to a trader's long-term success. Instead of focusing on the number of trades executed, traders

should prioritize the quality of each trade, ensuring that they meet predetermined criteria and offer favorable risk-reward prospects. Rule K encourages traders to resist the temptation to force trades and instead wait for setups that meet their standards and have a high probability of success.

3. *Risk Management*: Forcing trades often results in elevated risk levels, as traders may enter positions without proper risk assessment or consideration of market conditions. Rule K emphasizes the importance of risk management and preserving capital by avoiding unnecessary and impulsive trades. By exercising patience and waiting for optimal trading opportunities, traders can minimize risk exposure and protect their trading capital from unnecessary drawdowns.

4. *Maintaining Objectivity*: Forcing trades is often driven by emotions such as fear of missing out (FOMO) or a desire for instant gratification. Rule K encourages traders to maintain objectivity and rationality in their decision-making process, regardless of external influences or market fluctuations. By adhering to a disciplined trading approach based on analysis and strategy, traders can avoid emotional trading and make decisions that are consistent with their long-term goals and objectives.

Conclusion

Rule K – Never ever force a trade – underscores the importance of patience, discipline, and risk management in trading. By avoiding impulsive and unnecessary trades, traders can prioritize quality over quantity, minimize risk exposure, and maintain objectivity in their decision-making process. This disciplined approach fosters consistency, resilience, and long-term success in navigating the challenges of the financial markets.

Here are some quick and insightful **tips** derived from each trading rule that YOU can implement immediately:

K. Never ever force a trade:

- *Wait for high-probability setups that align with your trading strategy and have a clear rationale behind them.*

- *Be patient and disciplined; avoid FOMO (fear of missing out) and resist the urge to enter trades impulsively.*

L. There is no need for Fear Of Missing Out (FOMO).

As Jack's trading journey unfolded, he grappled with feelings of FOMO – the fear that he might miss out on lucrative trading opportunities. However, he soon learned to overcome this fear by adopting a patient and disciplined approach to his trading. By trusting in his analysis and waiting for the right setups to emerge, Jack realized that there was no need to rush into trades out of fear of missing out. Instead, he focused on quality over quantity and allowed the markets to come to him.

Exploration

1. *Emotional Discipline*: Rule L addresses the psychological phenomenon known as Fear Of Missing Out (FOMO), which can lead traders to make impulsive and irrational decisions. FOMO occurs when traders feel anxious or apprehensive about missing out on potential profits or opportunities in the market. This fear can compel traders to enter trades hastily without proper analysis or risk management. Rule L reminds traders to maintain emotional discipline and avoid succumbing to FOMO, as it often leads to poor trading decisions and unnecessary losses.

2. *Staying True to Strategy*: FOMO can cause traders to deviate from their established trading strategy and abandon their disciplined approach. Instead of following a systematic plan based on analysis and risk management, traders driven by FOMO may chase after trades that do not align with their strategy or criteria. Rule L emphasizes the importance of staying true to one's trading strategy and resisting the urge to act impulsively out of fear of missing out. By adhering to a well-defined plan, traders can maintain consistency and avoid the pitfalls of FOMO-driven trading.

3. *Patience and Selectivity*: Rule L encourages traders to exercise patience and selectivity in their trading activities, rather than acting impulsively based on FOMO. Instead of rushing into trades at the first sign of opportunity, traders should wait for setups that meet their criteria and offer favorable risk-reward prospects. By being patient and selective, traders can avoid falling victim to FOMO and focus on executing high-probability trades that align with their long-term goals and objectives.

4. Mindful Decision-Making: Overcoming FOMO requires traders to cultivate mindfulness and self-awareness in their trading approach. Rule L prompts traders to reflect on their emotions and thought processes, allowing them to recognize and address feelings of

FOMO before they lead to impulsive actions. By practicing mindfulness and maintaining a disciplined mindset, traders can make more deliberate and rational decisions in the face of market uncertainty and volatility.

Conclusion

Rule L – There is no need for Fear Of Missing Out (FOMO) – underscores the importance of emotional discipline, patience, and mindfulness in trading. By overcoming the urge to act impulsively out of FOMO, traders can maintain consistency, stick to their trading strategy, and avoid unnecessary losses. This disciplined approach fosters resilience and long-term success in navigating the challenges of the financial markets.

Here are some quick and insightful **tips** derived from each trading rule that YOU can implement immediately:

L. There is no need for Fear Of Missing Out:

- *Trust in your trading plan and wait for opportunities that meet your criteria rather than chasing after every market move.*

- *Focus on quality over quantity, and prioritize consistency in your trading approach.*

M. Write your trades down in a journal.

Throughout his trading journey, Jack recognized the importance of keeping a trading journal to track his progress and learn from his experiences. By documenting his trades – including entry and exit points, reasons for entering the trade, and lessons learned – Jack gained valuable insights into his strengths and weaknesses as a trader. This reflective practice helped him refine his trading strategy and become more disciplined and consistent in his approach.

Exploration

1. *Record-Keeping and Accountability*: Rule M emphasizes the importance of maintaining a trading journal to record and track all trading activities. A trading journal serves as a comprehensive record of trades, including entry and exit points, position size, reasons for trade entries, and outcomes. By documenting trades in a journal, traders hold themselves accountable for their decisions and actions, fostering transparency and self-awareness in their trading journey.

2. *Learning and Reflection*: Keeping a trading journal allows traders to learn from their experiences and reflect on their trading performance. By reviewing past trades, traders can identify

patterns, strengths, and areas for improvement in their trading approach. Journaling facilitates continuous learning and development, enabling traders to refine their strategies, adjust their behavior, and evolve as traders over time.

3. *Analyzing Trade Data*: A trading journal provides valuable data for analyzing trade outcomes and evaluating trading strategies. By aggregating trade data over time, traders can identify trends, assess the effectiveness of different trading approaches, and make data-driven decisions. Journaling enables traders to gain insights into their trading performance, risk management practices, and overall profitability, empowering them to make informed adjustments to their strategies.

4. *Emotional Management*: Writing down trades in a journal helps traders manage their emotions and maintain a disciplined mindset. By documenting trade entries, exits, and rationale, traders can detach themselves from the emotional rollercoaster of trading and focus on objective analysis. Journaling encourages traders to reflect on their emotions and thought processes, allowing them to make more rational and disciplined decisions in the heat of the moment.

Conclusion

Rule M – Write your trades down in a journal – underscores the importance of record-keeping, learning, and emotional management in trading. By maintaining a trading journal, traders create a valuable tool for accountability, learning, and analysis. Journaling facilitates continuous improvement, enhances self-awareness, and promotes disciplined decision-making, ultimately contributing to long-term success and growth as a trader.

Here are some quick and insightful **tips** derived from each trading rule that YOU can implement immediately:

M. Write your trades down in a journal:

- *Keep a detailed trading journal to record your trade setups, entry and exit points, rationale behind each trade, and emotions experienced.*

- *Review your trading journal regularly to identify patterns, strengths, and areas for improvement in your trading performance.*

N. Exercise before you enter the market.

While Jack's story didn't explicitly address the importance of exercise before entering the market, the concept of physical and mental well-being can still be applied. By prioritizing exercise and maintaining a healthy lifestyle, traders like Jack can enhance their focus, concentration, and decision-making skills. Regular exercise can also help reduce stress and anxiety, enabling traders to approach the markets with a clear and focused mindset.

Exploration

1. *Physical and Mental Well-being*: Rule N highlights the importance of physical exercise as a means of enhancing both physical and mental well-being before engaging in trading activities. Exercise has been shown to boost mood, reduce stress, and improve cognitive function, all of which are crucial for maintaining peak performance in trading. By incorporating exercise into their routine, traders can promote overall health and vitality, which can positively impact their trading mindset and decision-making.

2. *Stress Reduction*: Trading can be mentally demanding and stressful, especially during volatile market conditions. Exercise serves as a natural stress reliever, helping traders manage anxiety

and tension before entering the market. Physical activity triggers the release of endorphins, neurotransmitters that promote feelings of happiness and relaxation, thereby reducing the negative effects of stress on trading performance. Rule N encourages traders to incorporate exercise into their pre-trading routine to mitigate stress and promote emotional resilience.

3. *Enhanced Focus and Concentration*: Engaging in physical exercise before trading can also improve focus, concentration, and cognitive function. Exercise increases blood flow to the brain, delivering oxygen and nutrients essential for optimal mental performance. Additionally, physical activity stimulates the production of neurotransmitters like dopamine and norepinephrine, which are associated with improved attention and alertness. By preparing both the body and mind through exercise, traders can enhance their ability to stay focused and make clear-headed decisions in the fast-paced environment of the market.

4. *Setting a Positive Tone*: Incorporating exercise into the pre-trading routine sets a positive tone for the trading day ahead. Starting the day with physical activity can boost energy levels, motivation, and confidence, setting traders up for success in their trading endeavors. Rule N encourages traders to prioritize

self-care and well-being by making exercise a non-negotiable part of their pre-trading ritual, thereby fostering a positive mindset and readiness to tackle the challenges of the market.

Conclusion

Rule N – Exercise before you enter the market – underscores the importance of physical well-being and stress management in trading. By incorporating exercise into their pre-trading routine, traders can reduce stress, enhance focus and concentration, and set a positive tone for the trading day ahead. This disciplined approach to self-care promotes overall health and vitality, ultimately contributing to improved trading performance and well-being.

Here are some quick and insightful **tips** derived from each trading rule that YOU can implement immediately:

N. Exercise before you enter the market:

- *Incorporate physical activity or exercise into your daily routine before trading to improve focus, mental clarity, and overall well-being.*

- Even a brief workout or stretching session can help reduce stress and increase energy levels before engaging in trading activities.

O. Read your fundamentals every Sunday.

As Jack's trading journey progressed, he recognized the value of staying informed about fundamental factors that could impact the markets. While he may not have followed a specific routine of reading fundamentals every Sunday, Jack understood the importance of staying up-to-date with economic news, geopolitical events, and market developments. By staying informed, Jack was better equipped to make informed trading decisions and adapt to changing market conditions.

Exploration

1. *Staying Informed*: Rule O emphasizes the importance of staying informed about fundamental factors that drive the financial markets. Fundamental analysis involves assessing economic indicators, central bank policies, geopolitical events, and other macroeconomic factors that influence asset prices. By dedicating time to review fundamentals every Sunday, traders stay abreast of key developments and events that may impact their trading decisions in the week ahead.

2. *Understanding Market Context*: Fundamental analysis provides traders with a broader understanding of the underlying forces shaping market trends and movements. By examining economic

data releases, geopolitical tensions, and monetary policy decisions, traders gain insights into market sentiment, risk appetite, and potential market drivers. Rule O encourages traders to contextualize their technical analysis within the broader fundamental landscape, enabling them to make more informed and nuanced trading decisions.

3. *Anticipating Market Reactions*: Fundamental analysis allows traders to anticipate and prepare for market reactions to significant events and announcements. By forecasting how economic data releases or geopolitical developments may influence investor sentiment and market volatility, traders can adjust their trading strategies and risk management approaches accordingly. Rule O prompts traders to proactively assess the potential impact of upcoming events on their trading positions and portfolio.

4. *Long-Term Planning*: Reading fundamentals every Sunday facilitates long-term planning and strategic decision-making in trading. By staying informed about macroeconomic trends and structural shifts in the global economy, traders can identify emerging opportunities and risks that may affect their trading over the medium to long term. Rule O encourages traders to take a proactive approach to fundamental analysis, incorporating it into

their weekly routine to inform their trading strategies and investment decisions.

Conclusion

Rule O – Read your fundamentals every Sunday – underscores the importance of fundamental analysis and staying informed about macroeconomic factors in trading. By dedicating time each week to review economic indicators, central bank policies, and geopolitical events, traders gain insights into market dynamics, anticipate potential market reactions, and make more informed trading decisions. This disciplined approach to fundamental analysis enhances traders' understanding of market trends and drivers, ultimately contributing to improved trading performance and risk management.

Here are some quick and insightful **tips** derived from each trading rule that YOU can implement immediately:

O. Read your fundamentals every Sunday:

- *Dedicate time each Sunday to review economic calendars, news updates, and fundamental analysis reports relevant to your trading instruments.*

- Stay informed about upcoming events and developments that may impact the financial markets in the week ahead.

P. Wait for a confirmation before you enter.

In Jack's adventure, he learned the importance of patience and waiting for confirmation before entering a trade. While he may have initially been tempted to enter trades impulsively, Jack soon realized that waiting for confirmation – such as a breakout, trend reversal, or signal from his trading strategy – increased the probability of success. By exercising patience and discipline, Jack avoided jumping into trades prematurely and improved his overall trading performance..

Exploration

1. *Confirmation of Trade Setup*: Rule P emphasizes the importance of waiting for confirmation before entering a trade. Confirmation involves validating a trade setup with additional signals or criteria that support the trading decision. By waiting for confirmation, traders seek to increase the reliability and validity of their trade entries, reducing the likelihood of false signals and minimizing the risk of entering premature or low-probability trades.

2. *Technical Analysis*: In technical analysis, confirmation often involves waiting for price action to confirm a particular pattern or signal. For example, traders may wait for a candlestick pattern to close or for a breakout above a key resistance level before

entering a trade. By requiring confirmation from technical indicators or patterns, traders ensure that the market is validating their trade hypothesis before committing capital.

3. *Multiple Timeframe Analysis*: Confirmation can also be sought through multiple timeframe analysis, where traders assess the alignment of signals across different timeframes. For instance, a trader may look for confluence between signals on the daily and hourly charts before entering a trade. By confirming signals across multiple timeframes, traders increase the robustness of their trade setups and reduce the likelihood of entering trades based on temporary price fluctuations.

4. *Fundamental Validation*: In addition to technical confirmation, traders may also seek validation from fundamental factors before entering a trade. This could involve waiting for an economic data release to confirm the direction of a currency pair or assessing the impact of a geopolitical event on a particular asset. By incorporating fundamental analysis into the confirmation process, traders ensure that their trades are supported by a comprehensive understanding of market fundamentals.

Conclusion

Rule P – Wait for a confirmation before you enter – underscores the importance of patience and validation in trading. By waiting for confirmation from technical indicators, price action, or fundamental factors, traders increase the reliability and validity of their trade setups, reducing the risk of entering premature or low-probability trades. This disciplined approach to trade entry promotes consistency and improves the overall quality of trading decisions.

Here are some quick and insightful **tips** derived from each trading rule that YOU can implement immediately:

P. Wait for a confirmation before you enter:

- Confirm trade setups with multiple technical indicators, chart patterns, or fundamental factors before entering a position.

- Patience is key; wait for strong confirmation signals that increase the reliability of your trade setup.

Q. Have more than one strategy in your toolbox.

As Jack continued his trading journey, he discovered the value of having multiple trading strategies in his toolbox. While he may have started with a single approach or technique, Jack soon realized that different market conditions required different strategies. By diversifying his toolkit and adapting to various market environments, Jack became a more versatile and resilient trader, capable of navigating a wide range of scenarios with confidence and skill.

Exploration

1. **Diversification of Approaches**: Rule Q advocates for diversifying trading strategies to adapt to different market conditions and scenarios. Markets are dynamic and ever-changing, presenting varying trends, volatility levels, and trading opportunities over time. By having more than one strategy in their toolbox, traders can effectively navigate different market environments and capitalize on a broader range of trading opportunities.

2. **Flexibility and Adaptability**: Having multiple trading strategies allows traders to remain flexible and adaptable in their approach. What works well in one market condition may not perform as

effectively in another. By diversifying strategies, traders can switch between approaches based on prevailing market dynamics, optimizing their trading performance and adapting to changing circumstances as needed.

3. *Risk Management*: Diversifying trading strategies also contributes to effective risk management. Different strategies may have varying levels of risk and drawdown potential. By spreading risk across multiple strategies, traders reduce their exposure to any single strategy's performance and mitigate the impact of losses in one area of their trading portfolio. This diversified approach helps safeguard trading capital and preserve long-term profitability.

4. *Continuous Improvement*: Maintaining multiple strategies encourages traders to continuously refine and improve their trading skills. By experimenting with different approaches, traders gain valuable insights into market behavior, refine their trading methodologies, and evolve as traders over time. This ongoing process of learning and adaptation enhances traders' ability to navigate diverse market conditions and achieve consistent results.

Conclusion

Rule Q – Have more than one strategy in your toolbox – emphasizes the importance of diversification and adaptability in trading. By incorporating multiple strategies into their trading arsenal, traders can navigate different market conditions, manage risk effectively, and continuously improve their trading performance. This diversified approach fosters resilience, flexibility, and long-term success in the dynamic and competitive landscape of the financial markets.

Here are some quick and insightful **tips** derived from each trading rule that YOU can implement immediately:

Q. Have more than one strategy in your toolbox:

- Develop proficiency in multiple trading strategies suited to different market conditions, timeframes, and asset classes.

- Adapt your trading approach based on prevailing market dynamics and deploy the most appropriate strategy for each situation.

R. DO NOT BE GREEDY.

In Jack's story, he encountered moments of temptation and greed – the desire to maximize profits at all costs. However, he soon learned the dangers of greed and the importance of exercising restraint in his trading. By setting realistic profit targets and adhering to his trading plan, Jack avoided the trap of greed and focused on consistent, sustainable growth in the markets.

Exploration

1. *Risk of Overreaching*: Rule R addresses the detrimental effects of greed on trading performance. Greed can lead traders to overreach, taking excessive risks or deviating from their trading plan in pursuit of higher profits. This behavior often results in poor decision-making and increased vulnerability to losses. Rule R reminds traders to exercise restraint and avoid succumbing to the allure of greed, as it can undermine their long-term success in the markets.

2. *Maintaining Discipline:* Greed can erode discipline and rationality in trading, leading to impulsive actions and emotional decision-making. When driven by greed, traders may abandon their risk management principles, ignore warning signs, or chase after unrealistic profit targets. Rule R emphasizes the importance

of maintaining discipline and adhering to a structured trading plan, even when faced with the temptation of greed. By staying disciplined, traders can mitigate the negative impact of greed on their trading performance and preserve their capital.

3. *Setting Realistic Goals*: Greed often arises from unrealistic expectations or a desire for quick and easy profits. Rule R encourages traders to set realistic and achievable goals based on their trading strategy, risk tolerance, and market conditions. By setting clear objectives and aligning expectations with reality, traders can avoid falling victim to the pitfalls of greed and focus on consistent, sustainable growth in their trading endeavors.

4. *Cultivating Gratitude*: Overcoming greed requires cultivating gratitude and appreciation for what one already has achieved in trading. Instead of constantly chasing after more profits, traders can practice gratitude for their successes, no matter how small, and acknowledge the value of patience and perseverance in the journey toward long-term success. Rule R reminds traders to maintain a balanced perspective and avoid letting greed overshadow their appreciation for the progress they have made.

Conclusion

Rule R – DO NOT BE GREEDY – underscores the importance of discipline, realism, and gratitude in trading. By resisting the temptation of greed and maintaining a disciplined approach to trading, traders can safeguard their capital, mitigate risk, and pursue sustainable growth in the markets. This disciplined mindset fosters resilience, humility, and long-term success, ensuring that traders can navigate the challenges of the financial markets with confidence and integrity.

Here are some quick and insightful **tips** derived from each trading rule that YOU can implement immediately:

R. DO NOT BE GREEDY:

- *Set realistic profit targets and avoid chasing after unrealistic gains.*

- *Practice gratitude for profitable trades and focus on consistent, sustainable growth rather than excessive risk-taking or greed-driven behavior.*

S. If you win a trade at 3%, call it a day.

While Jack's story didn't explicitly address the rule of calling it a week after achieving a certain profit target, the concept of taking profits and celebrating success can still be applied. By recognizing when to step back and enjoy the fruits of his labor, Jack avoided the temptation to overtrade and maintained a healthy work-life balance. Celebrating small victories along the way helped Jack stay motivated and focused on his long-term goals in trading.

Exploration

1. *Locking in Profits*: Rule S advocates for disciplined profit-taking and risk management by setting a specific profit target for each trading session. When a trade reaches a profit of 3%, traders are encouraged to close the position and end their trading activities for the day. By locking in profits at this predetermined level, traders avoid the temptation to overtrade or give back gains, ensuring that they preserve their profitability and protect their capital.

2. *Avoiding Overconfidence*: Allowing winning trades to run indefinitely can lead to overconfidence and complacency, as traders may become overly optimistic about their ability to continue profiting from the market. Rule S helps mitigate this risk

by imposing a cap on profits for each trading session, regardless of market conditions or perceived opportunities. By adhering to this rule, traders remain grounded and disciplined, avoiding the pitfalls of overconfidence and maintaining a realistic perspective on their trading performance.

3. *Maintaining Balance*: Setting a profit target at 3% encourages traders to strike a balance between ambition and prudence in their trading approach. While it's essential to aim for profitable outcomes, it's equally important to recognize the limitations of each trading session and avoid excessive risk-taking in pursuit of higher gains. Rule S provides a clear guideline for traders to exit the market once they have achieved a reasonable level of profitability, helping them manage risk and preserve capital over the long term.

4. *Promoting Consistency*: Consistency is a hallmark of successful trading, and Rule S contributes to this by promoting consistent profit-taking behavior. By calling it a day after achieving a 3% profit, traders establish a routine of disciplined trading that reinforces positive habits and reinforces their commitment to risk management. Consistent adherence to this rule helps traders build confidence in their ability to achieve their trading goals while

mitigating the impact of adverse market conditions or unexpected events.

Conclusion

Rule S – If you win a trade at 3%, call it a day – emphasizes the importance of disciplined profit-taking and risk management in trading. By setting a specific profit target for each trading session and adhering to it rigorously, traders can lock in gains, avoid overtrading, and maintain consistency in their trading performance. This disciplined approach fosters resilience, discipline, and long-term success in the challenging and dynamic environment of the financial markets.

Here are some quick and insightful tips derived from each trading rule that YOU can implement immediately:

S.If you win a trade at 3%, call it a day:

- Take profits when they reach the predetermined target, and resist the urge to overtrade or give back gains.

- Ending the trading day on a high note reinforces discipline and helps maintain a positive mindset for future trading sessions.

T. Move your Stop Loss to breakeven after close above Take Profit

In Jack's journey, he encountered the challenge of managing his trades effectively and protecting his profits. While he may not have implemented the specific strategy of moving his Stop Loss (SL) to breakeven after hitting TP1, the concept of trailing stops to lock in profits can still be applied. By adapting his approach to trade management and protecting his gains, Jack minimized his risk and maximized his potential returns in the markets.

Exploration

1. *Protecting Profits*: Rule T aims to protect profits and reduce the risk of losses by implementing a breakeven stop loss strategy. Once a trade reaches Take Profit 1 (TP1), traders move their stop loss to the breakeven point, ensuring that the trade is no longer susceptible to incurring losses. This proactive approach helps traders secure profits and mitigate the potential impact of market reversals or adverse price movements.

2. *Risk Management*: Implementing a breakeven stop loss strategy enhances risk management and capital preservation in trading. By moving the stop loss to breakeven after achieving TP1, traders eliminate the risk of losing the profits already gained from the

trade. This risk-free position allows traders to participate in further upside potential while protecting their initial investment, thereby optimizing risk-reward dynamics and maintaining a favorable risk profile.

3. *Emotional Stability*: Rule T promotes emotional stability and confidence in trading by reducing uncertainty and anxiety associated with open positions. Once the stop loss is moved to breakeven, traders can trade with a sense of security, knowing that they have locked in profits and minimized the risk of incurring losses on the trade. This psychological reassurance enables traders to stick to their trading plan and remain disciplined in their decision-making process.

4. *Maximizing Profit Potential*: By implementing a breakeven stop loss strategy, traders aim to maximize profit potential from winning trades while minimizing downside risk. Moving the stop loss to breakeven allows traders to stay in the trade with reduced risk exposure, potentially capturing additional profits if the market continues to move in their favor. This strategic approach enables traders to capitalize on favorable price movements while protecting their capital and ensuring consistent profitability over time.

Conclusion

Rule T – Move your Stop Loss to breakeven after close above Take Profit 1 – underscores the importance of protecting profits and managing risk in trading. By implementing a breakeven stop loss strategy, traders secure profits, mitigate losses, and enhance emotional stability in their trading activities. This disciplined approach fosters confidence, consistency, and long-term success in navigating the challenges of the financial markets.

Here are some quick and insightful tips derived from each trading rule that YOU can implement immediately:

T. Move your Stop Loss to breakeven after close above TP1:

- Once your trade reaches Take Profit 1, move your stop loss to the breakeven point to secure profits and reduce risk.

- This strategy protects your initial investment and allows you to ride potential further price movements without risking previous gains.

U. Have more than one confirmation, always!.

As Jack honed his trading skills, he realized the importance of seeking multiple confirmations before entering a trade. While he may have initially relied on a single indicator or signal, Jack soon understood that combining multiple sources of confirmation – such as technical indicators, chart patterns, and fundamental analysis – increased the reliability of his trades. By conducting thorough analysis and seeking confirmation from different sources, Jack improved his decision-making process and enhanced his trading performance.

Exploration

1. *Enhancing Confidence*: Rule U emphasizes the importance of seeking multiple confirmations before entering a trade to enhance confidence in the trading decision. Having more than one confirmation validates the trade setup and reduces the likelihood of entering false or premature trades. Traders can gain greater assurance in their analysis and increase their conviction in executing the trade when multiple signals or criteria align.

2. *Risk Reduction*: Seeking multiple confirmations contributes to effective risk management by reducing the likelihood of false signals and minimizing the risk of losses. Each confirmation adds

an additional layer of validation to the trade setup, making it less susceptible to adverse market movements or unexpected events. By requiring multiple confirmations, traders can filter out low-probability trades and focus on high-confidence setups with favorable risk-reward profiles.

3. *Confirmation Diversity*: Rule U encourages traders to seek confirmation from different sources or indicators to ensure diversity in their analysis. This approach helps traders avoid over-reliance on any single signal or indicator, which may be subject to individual biases or limitations. By incorporating diverse confirmations from various technical and fundamental factors, traders can gain a more comprehensive understanding of the market dynamics and make more well-rounded trading decisions.

4. *Validation of Trading Strategy*: Seeking multiple confirmations validates the effectiveness of the trading strategy and enhances its robustness over time. When multiple signals or criteria align to support a trade setup, it reinforces the validity of the underlying trading methodology. Traders can gain confidence in their strategy's ability to identify high-probability trades and adapt to different market conditions by consistently seeking multiple confirmations before entering trades.

Conclusion

Rule U – Have more than one confirmation, always! – underscores the importance of seeking multiple confirmations to validate trade setups and enhance confidence in trading decisions. By requiring confirmation from diverse sources and indicators, traders can reduce risk, improve the effectiveness of their trading strategy, and enhance their overall trading performance. This disciplined approach fosters resilience, confidence, and long-term success in navigating the dynamic and challenging landscape of the financial markets.

Here are some quick and insightful tips derived from each trading rule that YOU can implement immediately:

U. Have more than one confirmation, always!:

- *Seek confirmation from multiple technical indicators, chart patterns, or fundamental factors before entering a trade.*

- *Confirming your trade setup with multiple sources increases confidence and reduces the likelihood of false signals.*

V. Only enter on the 15M timeframe.

While Jack's story didn't explicitly focus on trading within a specific timeframe, the concept of finding a suitable timeframe for one's trading style and strategy can still be applied. Whether Jack preferred shorter timeframes like the 15-minute chart or longer timeframes like the daily chart, the key was to find a timeframe that aligned with his trading goals, personality, and lifestyle. By choosing a timeframe that suited his needs, Jack optimized his trading experience and maximized his chances of success in the markets.

Exploration

1. *Timeframe Selection*: Rule V specifies the 15-minute (15M) timeframe as the primary timeframe for entering trades. The choice of timeframe can significantly impact trading decisions, as different timeframes offer unique perspectives on price action and market dynamics. The 15M timeframe strikes a balance between capturing short-term price movements and providing sufficient context for analysis, making it suitable for intraday trading strategies.

2. *Precision and Timing*: Trading on the 15M timeframe allows traders to capitalize on short-term price fluctuations with precision and timing. This timeframe provides enough granularity to identify

entry and exit points based on technical indicators, chart patterns, and price action signals. Traders can leverage the relatively rapid pace of price movements on the 15M timeframe to execute trades efficiently and take advantage of intraday opportunities.

3. *Reduced Noise*: The 15M timeframe filters out some of the noise and volatility present in shorter timeframes, such as the 5-minute or 1-minute charts, while still capturing meaningful price movements. By focusing on the 15M timeframe, traders can avoid getting caught up in minor price fluctuations and false signals that may distract from the overall market trend. This clarity allows traders to make more informed and objective trading decisions.

4. *Suitability for Intraday Trading*: Trading on the 15M timeframe is particularly well-suited for intraday trading strategies, where positions are opened and closed within the same trading session. The 15M timeframe provides enough granularity to capture intraday trends and reversals while allowing traders to manage risk and position sizes effectively. Traders who prefer intraday trading can benefit from the increased trading opportunities and liquidity available on the 15M timeframe.

Conclusion

Rule V – Only enter on the 15M timeframe – highlights the importance of timeframe selection in trading and emphasizes the advantages of focusing on the 15M timeframe for intraday trading strategies. By trading on the 15M timeframe, traders can benefit from precision, reduced noise, and suitability for intraday trading, enhancing their ability to identify and capitalize on short-term price movements in the market.

Here are some quick and insightful tips derived from each trading rule that YOU can implement immediately:

V. Only enter in the 15M timeframe:

- *Focus on trading on the 15-minute timeframe to capture short-term price movements and intraday trends.*

- *This timeframe strikes a balance between granularity and context, providing ample trading opportunities without overwhelming complexity.*

W. Remember, the trend is your friend., my friend!

In Jack's trading journey, he learned the timeless wisdom of following the trend and letting it guide his trading decisions. Whether he was trading stocks, forex, or other instruments, Jack understood that the trend was a powerful force that could lead to profits or losses. By aligning himself with the prevailing direction of the market, Jack embraced the mantra that "the trend is your friend" and leveraged it to his advantage in his trading endeavors.

Exploration

1. *Trend Identification*: Rule W underscores the importance of recognizing and trading in the direction of the prevailing market trend. The trend is a fundamental concept in technical analysis, representing the general direction in which prices are moving over time. By aligning with the trend, traders increase the probability of successful trades and reduce the risk of trading against the prevailing market momentum.

2. *Riding Market Momentum*: Trading with the trend allows traders to capitalize on market momentum and the collective behavior of market participants. Trends tend to persist over time, with prices moving in the direction of the dominant trend for extended periods. By riding the momentum of the trend, traders can capture

significant price movements and maximize their profit potential while minimizing the risk of counter-trend reversals.

3. *Risk Management*: Aligning with the trend also contributes to effective risk management by reducing the likelihood of entering trades against the prevailing market direction. Trading against the trend increases the risk of losses and requires tighter stop-loss levels to protect capital. By following Rule W and trading with the trend, traders can set wider stop-loss levels and give their trades more room to breathe, thereby reducing the risk of premature exits and maximizing the potential for profitable trades.

4. *Confirmation and Validation*: Rule W encourages traders to seek confirmation of the trend from multiple sources, such as trend indicators, moving averages, and trendline analysis. Confirming the trend helps validate the trading decision and provides additional confidence in the trade setup. By combining trend analysis with other technical and fundamental factors, traders can make more informed and well-rounded trading decisions that align with the prevailing market conditions.

Conclusion

Rule W – Remember, the trend is your friend., my friend! – emphasizes the importance of trading in the direction of the prevailing market trend. By aligning with the trend, traders can capitalize on market momentum, reduce the risk of losses, and increase the probability of successful trades. This disciplined approach to trend following fosters consistency, confidence, and long-term success in navigating the dynamic and ever-changing landscape of the financial markets.

Here are some quick and insightful tips derived from each trading rule that YOU can implement immediately:

W. Remember, the trend is your friend., my friend!:

- *Always trade in the direction of the prevailing market trend to increase the probability of successful trades.*

- *Use trend-following indicators and analysis to identify and capitalize on market momentum.*

X. Only trade when you are comfortable.

As Jack navigated the ups and downs of trading, he realized the importance of trading with confidence and conviction. While he may have experienced moments of doubt or uncertainty along the way, Jack learned to trust his instincts and only trade when he felt comfortable and prepared. By honoring his comfort zone and avoiding trades driven by fear or hesitation, Jack maintained a sense of control and clarity in his trading decisions.

Exploration

1. *Emotional Stability*: Rule X prioritizes emotional stability and well-being in trading by advocating for a comfortable trading environment. Trading can be emotionally demanding, and performing under stress or discomfort can impair decision-making and lead to poor outcomes. By trading only when comfortable, traders can maintain a clear and focused mindset, enabling them to make rational and disciplined trading decisions.

2. *Self-Awareness*: Trading when comfortable requires a high level of self-awareness and mindfulness. Traders must recognize their emotional state and physical condition before entering the market. If feeling stressed, anxious, or fatigued, traders may be more prone to making impulsive decisions or deviating from their trading

plan. Rule X encourages traders to assess their comfort level before trading and to prioritize self-care and well-being.

3. *Confidence in Strategy*: Trading comfortably also involves having confidence in one's trading strategy and approach. Traders should feel confident in their ability to analyze the market, identify high-probability trade setups, and execute trades according to their plan. If traders have doubts or uncertainties about their strategy, they may hesitate or second-guess their decisions, leading to missed opportunities or suboptimal outcomes.

4. *Risk Management*: Comfortable trading extends to risk management practices as well. Traders should only trade with capital they can afford to lose and implement appropriate risk management measures to protect their investment. If trading with excessive risk or uncertainty, traders may experience heightened stress and discomfort, negatively impacting their decision-making and overall trading performance.

Conclusion

Rule X – Only trade when you are comfortable – emphasizes the importance of prioritizing emotional stability, self-awareness, and confidence in trading. By trading in a comfortable and conducive environment, traders can maintain a clear and focused mindset, make rational decisions, and effectively manage risk. This disciplined approach to trading fosters resilience, consistency, and long-term success in the challenging and dynamic environment of the financial markets.

Here are some quick and insightful tips derived from each trading rule that YOU can implement immediately:

X. Only trade when you are comfortable:

- *Prioritize emotional stability and well-being by trading in a comfortable and conducive environment.*
- *Take breaks when feeling stressed or fatigued, and avoid trading under emotional duress.*

Y. Eat before you trade.

While Jack's story didn't explicitly address the importance of eating before trading, the concept of self-care and nourishment can still be applied. By prioritizing his physical and mental well-being, Jack ensured that he was in the best possible state to make informed decisions and manage his emotions effectively. Whether he enjoyed a hearty meal before trading or took regular breaks to refuel, Jack recognized the importance of taking care of himself to optimize his trading performance.

Exploration

1. *Physical Well-being*: Rule Y emphasizes the importance of nourishing the body and maintaining optimal physical health before engaging in trading activities. Eating before trading ensures that traders have the necessary energy and stamina to sustain focus and concentration throughout the trading session. Skipping meals or trading on an empty stomach can lead to fatigue, lack of concentration, and impaired decision-making, all of which can negatively impact trading performance.

2. *Blood Sugar Regulation*: Eating a balanced meal before trading helps regulate blood sugar levels and provides a steady source of

energy to the brain. Stable blood sugar levels are essential for maintaining cognitive function, alertness, and mental clarity, which are critical for making informed trading decisions. By fueling the body with nutritious foods, traders can optimize their cognitive performance and enhance their ability to analyze the market effectively.

3. *Emotional Regulation*: Eating before trading also plays a role in emotional regulation and stress management. Hunger and low blood sugar levels can exacerbate feelings of irritability, anxiety, and impulsivity, making traders more susceptible to emotional decision-making and reactive behavior. By nourishing the body with a nutritious meal, traders can stabilize their mood, reduce stress levels, and approach trading with a calm and composed mindset.

4. *Longevity and Sustainability*: Prioritizing proper nutrition and self-care before trading contributes to the long-term sustainability of a trader's career. Trading is a mentally demanding profession that requires consistent performance over extended periods. By adopting healthy eating habits and prioritizing physical well-being, traders can sustain their energy levels, maintain mental acuity, and withstand the rigors of the trading profession over the long term.

Conclusion

Rule Y – Eat before you trade – underscores the importance of prioritizing physical well-being and proper nutrition in trading. By fueling the body with nutritious foods before trading, traders can optimize cognitive function, regulate emotions, and sustain energy levels throughout the trading session. This disciplined approach to self-care promotes resilience, longevity, and sustainable success in the challenging and competitive landscape of the financial markets.

Here are some quick and insightful tips derived from each trading rule that YOU can implement immediately:

Y. Eat before you trade:

- *Nourish your body with a balanced meal before trading to maintain energy levels and cognitive function.*

- *Stable blood sugar levels help regulate mood and prevent impulsive decision-making during trading*

Z. Risk management is the most important rule.

In Jack's trading journey, he learned a valuable lesson that echoed throughout his adventures – risk management is the most important rule of all. Whether he was setting his risk per trade, managing his trades effectively, or knowing when to step back and take a break, Jack understood that!

Exploration

1. *Foundation of Trading*: Rule Z asserts that effective risk management serves as the cornerstone of successful trading. Regardless of the trading strategy or market conditions, risk management is paramount in preserving capital, mitigating losses, and safeguarding long-term profitability. Traders who prioritize risk management are better equipped to withstand market volatility, unexpected events, and adverse outcomes, ensuring the sustainability of their trading endeavors.

2. *Capital Preservation*: At its core, risk management is about preserving capital and protecting against the downside risk of trading. By implementing risk management techniques such as setting stop-loss orders, position sizing, and diversification, traders limit the potential loss on each trade and prevent catastrophic drawdowns that can wipe out trading accounts. Capital

preservation is essential for maintaining trading continuity and weathering periods of market uncertainty.

3. *Consistency and Discipline*: Effective risk management promotes consistency and discipline in trading. Traders who adhere to strict risk management principles maintain a structured approach to trading, avoiding impulsive decisions and emotional trading behavior. By consistently applying risk management rules, traders cultivate a disciplined mindset that fosters resilience, adaptability, and long-term success in the financial markets.

4. *Optimizing Risk-Reward*: Risk management is also about optimizing the risk-reward ratio of trades to maximize profitability. By carefully managing risk exposure and identifying high-probability trade setups with favorable risk-reward profiles, traders can achieve a balance between risk and reward that enhances their overall trading performance. Risk management allows traders to capitalize on profitable opportunities while minimizing the impact of potential losses, leading to consistent and sustainable returns over time.

Conclusion

Rule Z – Risk management is the most important rule – emphasizes the critical role of risk management in trading success. By prioritizing capital preservation, maintaining consistency and discipline, and optimizing risk-reward ratios, traders can effectively manage risk and enhance their long-term profitability in the financial markets. This disciplined approach to risk management forms the foundation of a resilient and sustainable trading strategy, ensuring that traders can navigate the challenges of trading with confidence and integrity.

Here are some quick and insightful tips derived from each trading rule that YOU can implement immediately:

Z.Risk management is the most important rule:

- Prioritize capital preservation and risk management above all else in your trading endeavors.

- Implement stop-loss orders, position sizing, and diversification strategies to mitigate losses and protect your trading capital.

By incorporating these tips into your trading routine, you can enhance your decision-making process, manage risk effectively, and increase the likelihood of long-term trading success. Remember to stay disciplined and consistent in applying these principles to your trading activities.

Conclusion

The journey through this book has been one of discovery, discipline, and development in the art and science of trading. As an artist from Nashville, Tennessee, with a background in drawing and graphic design, I've come to appreciate the similarities between creating art and navigating the financial markets. Both require a keen eye for detail, a steady hand, and a disciplined approach. This book is a culmination of the trading rules and principles that have guided me towards success in the foreign exchange market, particularly within the framework of a prop trading firm.

Purpose of This Book

The primary aim of this book is to equip you, the reader, with the essential rules and insights needed to navigate the complexities of trading with confidence and precision. Each rule, from risk management to the importance of trading within your designated session, is designed to help you cultivate a disciplined, consistent, and successful trading strategy. The tips and elaborations provided are practical and actionable, enabling you to implement them right away in your trading endeavors.

Trading, much like art, is a craft that requires continuous learning and adaptation. By adhering to these trading rules, you will not only protect your capital but also position yourself for sustained profitability and growth in the financial markets. Remember, the key to long-term success lies in the meticulous application of these principles, maintaining emotional stability, and always prioritizing risk management.

Explore Kreye Art Studio

Beyond trading, my passion for art and design continues to flourish. I'm excited to introduce my latest creations –

a designer backpack and a pair of tennis shoes that embody the fusion of art, design, and functionality. These unique pieces are now available for preorder and represent my artistic vision brought to life in everyday items. The designer backpack is crafted with precision, offering both style and practicality for your daily adventures. The tennis shoes are not only comfortable but also a statement of artistic expression, designed to stand out and complement your personal style.

How to order:

To order these exclusive items, visit Kreye Art Studio's website and navigate to the search bar section of the home page. Each piece is meticulously crafted and designed to enhance your lifestyle with a touch of artistic flair. Don't miss the opportunity to own these limited-edition items that combine creativity with functionality!

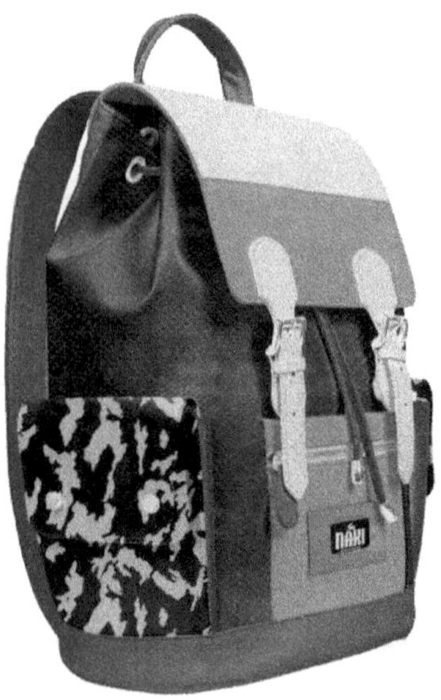

Trading Rules

Leave a Kind Review!

Your feedback is invaluable to us. If you've found this book helpful and are pleased with our products, I kindly request you to leave a positive review on Kreye Art Studio's Google page.

Your reviews not only help us improve but also assist other potential readers and customers in making informed decisions.

To leave a review, simply search for "Kreye Art Studio" on Google, click on our profile, and share your thoughts and experiences. Your support and kind words are greatly appreciated and help us continue to bring you valuable content and unique designs in the near future.

Final Thoughts

As you embark on your trading journey, remember that success is built on a foundation of discipline, continuous learning, and a steadfast commitment to your trading rules. This book is your guide, but your determination and adherence to these principles will ultimately shape your success. Thank you for taking this journey with me, and I wish you all the best in your trading and artistic endeavors.

Happy trading, and may your ***creative*** *and* ***financial ventures*** *flourish!*

THE END

www.ingramcontent.com/pod-product-compliance
Lightning Source LLC
LaVergne TN
LVHW082355200926
848481LV00012B/3575